21 Action Steps to Sales Success

VINIL RAMDEV

Published by

CEO Hangout, a Division of Zaang Entertainment Pvt Ltd
#48, St Johns Road, Bangalore 560042, India
www.ceohangout.com

This publication is designed to provide accurate and authoritative information about the subject matter. However, it is sold with the understanding that the publisher or the author is not engaged in providing professional services.

ISBN-13: 978-1542480277

ISBN-10: 1542480272

Copyright @ 2017 by Vinil Ramdev

All rights reserved. This book or any portion thereof may not be reproduced or used in any manner whatsoever without the express written permission of the publisher or author except for the use of brief quotations in a book review.

Limits of Liability/Disclaimer of Warranty: Although the author and publisher have made every effort to ensure that the information in this book was correct at press time, the author and publisher do not assume and hereby disclaim any liability to any party for any loss, damage, or disruption caused by errors or omissions, whether such errors or omissions result from negligence, accident, or any other cause.

Contents

Introduction 4

Intent 6

One Massive Ingredient to Success 10

Goal Setting and Productivity 16

Habits 20

Schedule 24

Target Market 28

Why do people buy? 31

The Sales Process 34

How to introduce yourself? 40

Presentation 44

Follow-up 50

Handling Objections 56

Closing 63

Creating Energy 69

Your Value 71

Offers 76

How to be a Master Networker 79

Breaking Mental Barriers 85

Referrals 88

Landing Pages 92

Habits of Successful Sales People 99

Conclusion 103

Index 105

INTRODUCTION

Sales can be very intimidating for some people. However, I've seen sales people who enjoy their jobs and have created lucrative careers for themselves.

Whether you are an entrepreneur, sales professional, or someone who's looking to better his salesmanship skills, you will find that this guide book is practical and encourages the reader to take action.

I still remember my very first sales job. I was still in college, and I responded to an ad in a newspaper. When I went for the interview, I realized that it was a door-to-door sales job. I decided to take the leap and soon realized sales can be quite enjoyable.

Later, I moved to the US for college, and I needed a job. So I took up jobs that were predominantly in sales and marketing.

My first internship was in sales and marketing; I worked for a non-profit where I had to call local businesses and ask them to donate funds for charity.

It turned out to be an exciting gig. Even though we were asking for charitable funding, we still had to find ways to appeal to people's emotions, rather than expecting them to help automatically. It was a challenge, but very rewarding.

Those are just some of the jobs I've had.

After that, I started a business and have been an entrepreneur ever since.

I've learned that one can't be a successful entrepreneur if one is not good at selling.

From hiring your first employee, to signing your first client, you are *always* selling.

The way this book is organized is that it has 21 action steps.

Each lesson is short and after each lesson there is an action step.

This book is organized in such a manner that you should take one action, each day, for 21 days.

Some people have gone through this book multiple times and have made each of these action steps into a habit. I encourage you to do the same.

Each of these action steps should become a habit that you implement automatically over time.

Wish you all the best!

Intent

The biggest challenge in today's world is building trust. I believe trust is the foundation of successful sales and business. All 12 years that I've been in business, and being an entrepreneur, I've seen that the number one reason for business failure is a lack of integrity.

Most good sales people spend the majority of their time building trust, and the rest of their time in presenting and closing deals. I believe integrity is an important value proposition to have. It is the foundation of all business. When you have integrity, you position yourself as a person who can be trusted and relied upon to make a good decision.

Recently, I was having a conversation with a friend of mine who said, "You have to be unethical and lie a lot if you want to be successful in sales." This is so far away from the truth. A lot of people have this perception about sales -- that sales people will do anything for a sale, including screwing your prospect over if you have to. I believe that's the wrong methodology and the wrong philosophy to have.

The most important thing about sales is to build a relationship. Your first job as a sales person is to build a relationship with your prospect. If you have a strong relationship with your prospect, you're going to have multiple sales over a period of time. Look at the lifetime value of a prospect. That's most important. The biggest reason most sales don't happen is due to a lack of trust.

I still remember a note that hung on the wall in the office of my first internship. It said, "You cannot make people trust you, but you can be trustworthy." If you think a specific product is not suitable for your prospect, you shouldn't recommend it. Suggest only those products and services that are beneficial to your prospect. Your intent should always be very clear. You should go into a sales meeting with the intention to benefit your prospect.

Warren Buffet once said, "We can afford to lose a lot of money but not our reputation." Before you get into any deal, I strongly encourage you to be clear about your values.

What are values? Values are a set of beliefs which dictate what is right or what is wrong. They form the framework of decision making.

You should live your principles everyday of your life and your entire decision making should be based on your values and principles. Some of us are conscious of our values, while others are not conscious about their values.

Most of your values are in your subconscious mind. It's important to bring it out into your conscious and be clear about them. If you believe that your values are not going to benefit you in life, change those values and bring in new values that are going to benefit you and make you a better person. Overall, your beliefs dictate your actions.

If you believe in something, you will rarely make decisions that go against your beliefs. On the rare occasions you do go against them, you will feel an inner conflict.

When we created an employee handbook for my company, I created a list of values for the kind of people we seek to attract. We mentioned in the handbook that people join our company not just for financial rewards, but for the learning experiences.

Once we created our core philosophy, we attracted people whose values matched that of ours. Even on a personal level, you will attract people who match your core philosophy, values and beliefs. If your values are not aligned with your product, the people and the company you're working with, you will always feel an inner emotional conflict. Therefore, I encourage you to become conscious of your values. And once you are conscious of your values, you will understand yourself, and others, better.

Action Step

Write down your values on a sheet of paper. Examples may include integrity, honesty, sincerity and showing up on time. Just write down whatever comes to mind.

Some people will write four or five sentences. Others will write just four or five words. And there are a few others who will write several pages. Don't judge yourself while you're writing — just write it down. Once you've written it down, you can always go back and polish it up.

When I did this exercise I wrote, "My value is to make a positive impact on every person I touch. I seek to help people who are genuinely interested in growing and becoming better people."

Notes:

One Massive Ingredient to Success

The topic in this chapter can dramatically change your life. I'm not talking about incremental results; I'm talking about a quantum leap. I call this self-image.

A friend of mine who's extremely competent and knowledgeable about her field of work isn't as successful as many other people in the same profession. Her competitors have far lesser knowledge than her, but they're still far more successful than her.

I couldn't figure that out initially. I looked at her and wondered, "Why isn't she as successful as other people even though she's got far more expertise than people who are successful in her profession?" I realized there's just one reason: her self-image. She has a very poor self-image about herself.

What is self-image? When I talk about self-image, I'm not talking about the reflection you see in the mirror. That's your external image. I'm talking about the image that is deeply rooted in your subconscious mind.

As kids when we were growing up, we're told a lot of things about ourselves. It could be from a teacher, a friend, a parent or a neighbor. Things like, "You won't amount to much in your life. You will not be successful in your life. You will not get ahead in your life. You're a loser. You're not good at what you do."

These are things we hear as children, and as kids we don't know what to make of it. Many of these thoughts get deposited in our subconscious mind. And when we grow up, it's probably still there in our subconscious mind and we're not even aware of it. We gain knowledge, we gain skills, but we still see less skilled people get ahead and do extremely well. There's only one reason: poor self-image.

There's this little story that I heard very early in my life. A very successful car sales person would convince his new hires to buy a Cadillac. This new hire would buy a Cadillac, he would drive it home and then his neighbors, family and friends would start looking at him differently. They're fascinated that this person has not only purchased a brand new car, but a *super* luxury car – the Cadillac.

Gradually, this new hire starts feeling more successful. His self-image begins to change. This is probably one of the many reasons why many talented, smart people don't get ahead in life – because they have a very poor self-image.

If you go to the gym, you may have noticed fat people working out and following a diet; for a brief moment you see that they lose weight, but sure enough they get back to being fat. What's the reason for that? They have a self-image of being a fat person. They think like a fat person. If they want to get slimmer, they need to change their mindset before it can physically manifest itself.

In the book, The Secret, the authors talk about focusing on what you want, rather than what you don't want.

Many of us focus on what we don't want. *We don't like the traffic. We don't like losing money.* Instead of thinking about the traffic or losing money, focus on something that you want. Focus on making more sales.

By focusing on what you want, your attention and your energy is channeled towards the positive, rather than the negative. If you want to be a sales person or an entrepreneur who's clocking 10 million dollars or 100 million dollars in sales, your self-image should reflect that. You must mentally feel like you're making millions of dollars in sales, before it can manifest itself physically.

When my team and I were running the exhibition business, we always made a certain number of sales. Every single event, our sales were similar and I wondered, "How do we break this barrier?" I realized my sales team and I had a self-image of being at that same level which ultimately hindered our ability to increase our sales.

We needed to change our self-image if we wanted to make more sales. If you want to get ahead, you need to make a mental image of attaining a higher number of sales. A lot of people are stuck at a certain level of sales, and the reason why they're stuck at a certain level of sales is because their mindset is stuck at that level. It really is that simple.

A friend of mine, who is a life coach, talks about positivity and says affirmations help you to change your inner story. Initially, I didn't believe in affirmations. I tried affirmations about 10 years ago when I was a lot younger. I don't know if they worked for me because my mind was very distracted. I didn't pay too much attention to it.

But then, this friend of mine explained it to me. He said, "Vinil, affirmations are about changing your inner story. And affirmations work when they're done right and consistently. The moment you hear anything negative, just tell yourself, 'I'm a positive person who can find solutions.'"

My friend also tells me to, "Make a list of all the positive things about yourself. You should start your day by saying these positive things."

Some examples are:

Prosperity is coming my way every day.
I am a good, humble and sensitive person.
I treat people with respect.
I am worthy of all the success that comes to me.
I will do whatever it takes to achieve prosperity and abundance in my life.
My life is worthy and purposeful.
I am a successful sales person.

Say these things to yourself every single day. I know a lot of you will be like, "Oh, come on, I can't *lie* to myself." But you believed all the lies that you were told as a kid. If you believed all the lies then, why can't you believe all the lies that you tell yourself as an adult? Initially, your inner voice will say, "Uh, come on, this is a lie." But then, you must keep fighting your inner voice and you will start saying, "I am a successful person."

Start creating a visual image of who you want to be. You have the power to create your own inner story.

The moment you change your self-image, magical things will start happening to you. I've experienced that in my own life, and I've seen it happen in the lives of many others as well. Whether you believe it or not, I encourage you to try it for at least 100 days.

Write down a set of affirmations. It could be as simple as, "I'm a positive person. I will do what it takes to make 10 million dollars in sales. I'm a successful sales person."

Say these affirmations every day.

Find something that you believe works for you. Write down these affirmations on a sheet of paper. Say them to yourself every single day for at least 100 days.

My friend who is a life coach charges people a lot of money just for affirmations. He says, "Vinil, you have to charge a lot of money when you coach people in affirmations."

And you know what his personal coaching clients do every day? They give him a call and they tell him these affirmations!

These affirmations are so powerful that they can change your life. And once you keep saying them to yourself, they begin to form your inner story.

You can practice visualization techniques as well. Sit down, close your eyes and visualize where you want to be.

You will attract the things that you want.

Imagine all of the world's greatest discoveries. Take the aircraft for example. Before the aircraft was made, if the Wright brothers walked up to someone and said, "Hey, I'm creating a machine that people are going to sit in, and it will fly them from one country to the other," people would have laughed at them. And yet, the Wright brothers still believed in it.

I encourage you to set big, audacious goals for yourself and visualize these goals coming to life every single day. Say positive things to yourself. Give yourself positive pep talks every day. If you are your own cheerleader, why do you need a cheerleader? You don't.

So, be your own cheerleader, cheer yourself up every day, say positive things about yourself and change your inner image. Make it into a bigger, more powerful inner image.

Action Step

Write down a list of affirmations. I know people who write one page, two page, and even three page affirmations.

You can use some of the affirmations I listed above, or you can create your own. Start your day by saying these things. It will put you in a positive frame of mind which is a fantastic way to start any day.

Notes:

Goal Setting and Productivity

A wise man once said, "No matter how slow or fast you are, every step you take should be towards your goal."

I see a lot of people get very excited when they set goals. The excitement lasts for a few days and then it tends to weather off.

The whole idea about goal setting is to keep you focused, because every action you take should be towards your goal.

That's what productivity is all about. If you don't have goals, you're going to be distracted, and, every day you're not going to know what to do and what not to do. Goals give you that focus; the focus to only put time into certain activities that help you to achieve your goals.

Darren Rowse of ProBlogger shared a very interesting concept called "micro ambition." A lot of people think too far ahead and Rowse believes people should focus on more short term successes.

I love long term goals. I look at goals from a 10 year horizon, five year horizon, and a two year horizon. But when we set long term goals, we tend to procrastinate.

We think, "Oh, it's five years down the line, I have plenty of time. I'll think about it another time." I challenge you to break them up into one year goals, quarterly goals, monthly, weekly and even daily goals.

I love daily goals because daily goals give you a focus every single day.

You wake up in the morning and you say, "By the end of today, I want to achieve this goal."

That is a micro ambition; you're ambitious for today. You're looking forward to today with excitement.

Look at your daily goals and say, "What is my goal for today? What do I need to get done today so I can make my tomorrow better?" That's what your daily goals do. They give you focus for the day.

And the moment you achieve something nice, I encourage you all to go and reward yourselves.

So every day if you're achieving goals, and you're rewarding yourself for achieving those goals, it makes you more excited about life in general. And every single day you're going to be seeing yourself making a little bit more progress.

I believe in making a little bit of progress every single day. One year down the line, you will have made so much progress that it would be hard for you to even believe it yourself!

One action a day for 365 days is 365 actions. That's a lot of work over a one year period. But when you break it down daily it becomes so much more attainable - fun, even!

I also believe that life is about making those little starts. I have friends of mine who are very successful, but when they're trying new things like embracing social media or learning to make videos, they want to start right at the top.

They want be the best on day one which is very impractical.

It's about making a *start*.

Your first video isn't going to be brilliant, your first football kick probably won't be a touchdown and your first day of swimming may not go, well, swimmingly.

You're going to be horrible at it initially, but if you make a start and do it repeatedly, then over a period of time you'll be much better at it.

Bruce Lee once said, "It's not about practicing a thousand kicks once. It's about practicing one kick a thousand times."

It means if you practice something long enough, you'll eventually be good at it. I see a lot of people struggle to make a start because they're scared that they may not be good enough.

Of course, you're not going to be good when you try something for the first time! But if you stick to it long enough, you're going to become good at it.

So, don't be scared to be imperfect.

Just make that start and enjoy every moment of that start. Sometimes it's nice to be a beginner. I am someone who tries many new things all the time. And as they say, "Life is not about the destination, it's the journey that matters."

It's time for us to embrace this journey, take one day at a time, and explore the destiny nature has scripted for us.

Action Step

Write down your goals for the year then break them up into quarterly goals, then monthly, weekly and, eventually, daily goals.

Then write down every single task you need to do to achieve that goal.

When you set daily goals, you'll be surprised to see how much you can achieve in a day!

Notes:

Habits

Sometimes, there are certain old habits that keep us from getting our desired results.

How do habits develop? Most of our habits are actually developed unconsciously. The brain is programmed way beforehand, and usually it's programmed unconsciously. We pick things up from our childhood, from our early adulthood, in our adolescence, and these things form habits and they become a part of us. If these habits do not help us, then we need to change these habits.

The first part of breaking away from these old habits is to become aware of them. Many of us are not even aware of our old habits.

There are two things that are very important – one is your technical skills, the other are your mental skills. If you're making sales of a hundred thousand dollars a year and you want to start making a million dollars in sales, or even 10 million dollars in sales, you need to understand a few things.

First, the mindset for making 10 million dollars a year in sales is different from a 100 thousand dollars a year in sales.

Many people who come to my workshop have the mental skills, but they want to develop the technical skills. And there are many others who have the technical skills, but don't have the mental skills.

One of my team members said she likes to work towards the evening, from 10PM to about 4AM. So I asked her, "Is this a productive activity for you, or is it unproductive?" She said, "It's unproductive. And over a period of time, I'm going to become really tired and burned out." I then asked her, "What do you do from morning till 10PM?" She says, "I don't know, I have no clue what I do from morning to evening."

Lots of people waste time on activities that are totally unproductive. Some of them are on social media which, by the way, is the biggest distraction for most people. Others are just reading articles online. Some of it is beneficial, some of it isn't. And many of us are chatting over on an instant messenger like WhatsApp, or with friends over the phone. We are predominantly doing unproductive activities.

I want you to do a little exercise now. Over the next day, make a list of all the activities that you do throughout the day; from the time that you wake up till the time you sleep.

Maintain a journal and write down every single activity that you've been doing. And then, next to each of these activities, list them as either having been productive or unproductive.

Some activities are outright unproductive and you may notice a pattern.

Sometimes, being on social media can be unproductive. But for some people who are social media marketers, who are connecting with people, for them, being on social media is productive.

So figure out what is productive and what is unproductive for you. List these activities on a sheet of paper.

Before listing your activities as productive or unproductive, make a list of goals for yourself.

What is it that you want to achieve in the next month, the next quarter or the next year – whatever works for you. Some people like to look at a one year horizon, others like to look for one quarter. A few others like to look at their weekly goals. See what works for you. If monthly goals work for you, write down your monthly goals.

And the way to figure out if a certain activity is productive or unproductive is by figuring out whether each of these activities is leading you towards your goal or not. If it's not leading you towards your goals, it's an unproductive activity.

If it's leading you towards your goals, it is a productive activity.

Make a list of these activities. Once you've made a list of these activities, your next challenge is to cut out unproductive activities from your life and focus only on your productive activities.

Very simple, right? But the simplest things are the hardest to implement.

If 80% of your time is focused on productive activities, you're going to reward yourself.

How are you going to reward yourself? You could buy yourself a chocolate, you can buy yourself an ice cream, a fruit juice, or you could go shopping, on a budget of course! Do anything that makes you happy.

Figure out what makes you happy. Figure out one activity that makes you happy. It could even be going for a movie. So, if in a specific day you complete 80% of your activities, you get to do one thing that you really enjoy.

This is the rewards mechanism.

Some people talk about the punishment mechanisms. What are punishment mechanisms? If you don't do something, you kind of punish yourself. I am not a big believer in the punishment system. I'm a big believer in the reward system. The moment you do something right, you reward yourself.

Researchers in Germany told a group of people the benefits of working out. Once they were told the benefits of working out, how many people do you think worked out?

Not that many as you may have guessed.

But when people were given a reward to work out, they started working out on a regular basis. Once people stopped getting the reward, did people stop working out? Not necessarily.

They continued working out because it had become a habit.

Action Step

Follow this mechanism and focus on your productive activities. And every single day, if you focus at least 80% of your time on your productive activities, you're going to reward yourself with one thing that you really enjoy.

Try this activity for at least 21 days.

Notes:

Schedule

Many of our lives and day-to-day activities run on autopilot, and we seldom stop to think if it's something that we've planned consciously, or if it's due to circumstances that have fostered it upon us.

Some of us have a certain randomness to our work schedule. Every day is different.

But by creating set patterns, we absolve ourselves from making repetitive decisions on a day-to-day basis, thereby increasing our overall productivity.

Patterns bring a sense of order and rhythm to our lives. In fact, that's what effective systems do for companies.

Decisions are made and thought through way beforehand.

Warren Buffet once said, "Never make a decision when you're tired. It's the worst time to make a decision."

In his book, Daily Rituals, Mason Currey mentions a quote from WH Auden – "Routine in an intelligent man is a sign of ambition."

He further quotes a guest of Auden's who once noted, "Eating, drinking, writing, shopping and crossword puzzles, even the mail man's arrival – all are aimed to the minute and with accompanying routines."

The book also mentions that Auden was an early riser and his cocktail hour usually started at 6:30 pm with strong vodka martinis. The great man never going to bed later than 11pm.

The book infers that great people had schedules that varied little over their entire lifetimes.

Another great artist, Francis Bacon, whose life appeared disorderly to the outside world with excessive alcohol consumption and late night parties, had a work pattern that varied very little over his entire lifetime.

Currey's book mentions that in spite of the late-night parties, Bacon rose early and worked for several hours usually finishing his work before noon.

Then another long afternoon and evening of carousing stretched before him.

He would have a friend to his studio to share a bottle of wine, followed by a long lunch at a restaurant, and then more drinks at the succession of private clubs. Seems like a fascinating life, doesn't it?

The single most productive activity that has gotten me results over my entire lifetime is to start my day at the exact same time.

I'm a great believer in having a consistent schedule.

If you go out of town for a business conference, a networking event or a vacation, your schedule changes for that brief period.

But when you're back, you're onto your normal schedule.

In short, plan your day beforehand and have a consistent schedule. Schedule enough time for sleep and to do something fun. When you do something for fun or for pleasure, your brain cells get activated.

And that's very important because you need to feed your spirit. If you're only working all the time, you'll probably reach a stage where you ask yourself, "Why am I doing all this? Is it even worth it?"

So it's very important to schedule enough time for pleasure.

Also schedule enough time for sleep, because an average adult requires at least seven hours of sleep. If you don't sleep well, you're going to get cranky and irritated, and it's not a sustainable schedule for a long period of time.

You need to have a schedule that's highly sustainable for your entire lifetime.

Besides sleep and play, you should schedule time for physical fitness.

Exercise releases endorphins in your body, which makes you happy. And happy, healthy, and energetic people tend to attract more people towards them.

And as sales people, you want to attract prospects towards you.

Action Step

Write down your schedule on a sheet of paper.

Here's a sample schedule. You can tweak it to fit your needs, or create a new one.

7 am to 8 am:	Gratitude, self-talk, preparing my attention list for the day.
8 am to 9 am:	Shower, breakfast.

21 Action Steps To Sales Success

9:30 am to 10 am:	Networking on social media.
10 am to 10:30 am:	Make a list of leads to call.
10:30 am to 11:30 am:	Tele-calling
12 pm to 1:30 pm:	Handling client work and assigning/delegating tasks to my team.
2:30 pm to 5 pm:	Meetings, marketing related activities
5 pm to 6 pm:	Reply to emails and other miscellaneous work
6:30 pm to 7:30 pm:	Workout

Notes:

Target Market

When I meet people, I tend to ask them, "Who is your target market?"

I get replies like, "My target market is *everybody*."

Guess what? If your target market is everybody, then it's really *nobody*.

I believe great sales people and great marketers know their target markets very well. By having a target market, your efforts are more strategic.

If you want to target men of a certain age group and you know where they hang out, it's easy for you to hang out in those places and get access to this target market.

It's just like goal setting. If you don't have a goal, then you don't know where you're going.

If you don't have a target market, you don't know who your ideal customer is, and you don't know how to reach them.

You can target a segment based on psychographics, demographics or your geography.

Psychographics is simply targeting a market based on the psychological attributes of a particular segment of people.

It could be based on attitudes, aspirations or a specific behavior the group shares.

Demographics is basically gender, age, marital status, family size, education and income level.

And geography is, of course, based on location.

A real estate agent, whom I know, targets people in his five-kilometer radius. That's it.

He's the go-to guy for any properties in that five-kilometer radius.

What are the advantages of having a target market?

The biggest advantage, of course, is that your efforts are strategic.

For example, if you're placing an ad on Facebook you can target people based on interest, demographics, job title, universities, etc. These are some of the areas where you can specifically target people.

In my business, we target predominantly business owners. We understand the needs of our target market better than those who are catering to many different markets.

Some of the common mistakes I see people make is that their sales copy or their pitch is the same for every single market segment.

I believe your sales copy should be slightly different for different audiences.

If you're targeting younger people, your sales copy is different. If you're targeting older people, your sales copy should be a little bit different. The language you use is very important to your potential clients.

Another mistake that I see sales people and marketers make is that they target people with no money or motivation to actually buy their product.

Imagine that you're selling a Rolls Royce in a low-income neighborhood. It would be nearly impossible for you to sell one, even if you're the greatest salesman in the world.

What I look for when I'm choosing a target market is an audience that has the money; they can afford my product, and they are already buying similar products.

I also look for some sort of unfair advantage over my competition.

It could be access to an audience or some special skill that only me and my organization has. So based on your skills, you could target a specific target market.

Action Step

Write down who your ideal customer is and then write down why your ideal customer would buy from you rather than your competition.

The more details you have about your ideal customer, the better. Identify his or her goals. Identify how these ideal customers will find you.

Notes:

Why do people buy?

Prospects buy primarily for two types of reasons; physical or emotional reasons.

People buy shampoo because it helps them stay clean. They buy food so they can survive. They buy water because they're thirsty. These are physical reasons.

But why do people buy Evian water compared to a cheaper brand?

People don't necessarily go to a restaurant to eat. They go there for the *ambiance*. They go there to feel good about themselves.

Why do people buy a Mercedes as opposed to a Toyota Corolla? Both take you from point A to point B. Some of you might argue comfort. But sometimes you see cheaper cars that are comfortable as well.

When people buy a Mercedes, they're not buying a car. They're buying a status symbol. When you become successful, you buy a Mercedes or a Cadillac or a Rolls Royce.

Prospects are buying *feelings*.

They are buying emotions.

When you sell your product, look at the feeling that you're selling.

Because we are all selling feelings, at the end of the day.

We need to look at logical reasons as well as emotional reasons – both are of equal importance. A lot of people look only at the logical reasons when they're selling a product.

They don't look at the emotional reasons.

Prospects buy products for a variety of reasons. To save time, to make them feel good about themselves, etc.

If people similar to them have purchased your product, they will want to purchase it too.

If my prospect is a small business owner and I tell him thousands of small business owners have purchased my product to save money, he's more likely to buy.

When you're presenting your product or service to your prospect, it's important to identify the feeling you're selling as well.

Buying insurance gives people the feeling of safety and security.

Action Step

Ask yourself the following questions:

Why do people buy your product as opposed to other products or services?
What is the logical and emotional reason?

Write them down on a sheet of paper.

Notes:

The Sales Process

I'd like to break up the sales process into seven steps.

Step 1: Lead Generation

Step 2: Introduction

Step 3: Qualification

Step 4: Presentation

Step 5: Follow-up

Step 6: Handling Objections

Step 7: Closing

In this chapter we'll talk about step one, lead generation. We'll cover the other steps in later chapters.

Experienced sales people will tell you that nothing happens unless you have a lead.

Without leads, there are no sales.

You need to have a bunch of interesting people who are willing to buy.

So, how do you generate leads?

As a business, you need to figure out where you are going to get your leads from.

Some of them advertise in the newspaper.

During the good old days, a B2B (business to business) sales person would just pick up the yellow pages and he would call a bunch of businesses from there.

But, today, sales has become a little more complex because there are more sellers than buyers in the market.

Sales people need to be a little bit more sophisticated with their selling.

The three main sources of leads for me has been social media, search engines and business conferences.

I attend a lot of business conferences and networking events.

Facebook and LinkedIn have also been good for me; I've been able to generate many leads from them.

Then there are Google advertisements.

More than 65% of search traffic comes from Google, so it makes sense to focus on the largest search engine.

I don't focus on too many search engines; I only focus of Google.

I've tried Yahoo! and Bing, but I haven't had as much success from them.

Let me explain how I generate leads from Facebook.

When you go onto Facebook and you click on 'create ad,' you'll see different types of ads that can be created.

Some increase traffic to your website, while others increase traffic to your events. What I like to focus on is the lead generation ad.

Yes, they have an ad just for generating leads!

So, on those lead generation ads, people can just enter their contact details and click 'submit.' Then, you can go on to the forms on Facebook and all your leads would be there.

You can download it in the form of an Excel sheet. This is what I use to generate leads.

Usually I give away something free, like an e-book.

Many of you can also give away reports or case studies.

If you have had clients who've been benefited from using your product, you can give away those case studies.

You can also ask them to schedule a demo for your product. These are all leads that are interested in your product.

Now, your job is to convert those interests into sales meetings.

On Facebook you can target people based on interests, location, age, and work titles. This is a fabulous way to target the right audience for your business.

The other method that I use are Google AdWords.

Sometimes you get good qualified leads from Google ads depending on your product and your target market.

When I place an ad using Google adverts, I usually get people on a landing page where people need to give me their information – their name, email, phone number, and they need to click on the 'submit' button.

That's how I get leads.

It's very important when people come on to your landing page for you to ask for their personal information.

When I say personal, I'm not talking about their social security number. Their name, email, and phone number is all you're looking for. I see a lot of websites that don't even ask people for their information -- how are you supposed to generate leads in that case?

It's very important to make sure you collect information from whatever marketing campaign you do.

LinkedIn is another very important tool that can be used to generate leads.

On LinkedIn, there is an option where you can sign up for a premium account and there's an option to send "inmail."

You can search for people based on company, job title, industry etc. If you're targeting someone predominantly in the B2B market like marketing managers, you can use LinkedIn to identify who they are, and you can send them inmails introducing yourself. You can say something like,

"Hello! I recently came across your profile and I think we can connect and explore mutual synergies."

The whole idea about LinkedIn is to get them onto a sales meeting.

You don't want to sell them online, but you want to get them onto a sales meeting.

Say, "Hey, you know what, can we just meet up sometime and connect to see how we can help each other out?"

Start off with a meeting that way.

LinkedIn is a great platform to connect with high profile professionals.

The next source of leads is business conferences.

There are so many meet-ups, business conferences and training programs happening all the time, all over the world.

You can find one in your local area and attend one of them.

The Chamber of Commerce is another place where you can go and meet people. These are places where you will meet people face-to-face. You have a distinct advantage when you meet people face-to-face.

I'm going to explain how to connect with people in business conferences in a later chapter.

If you look around you, you will find hundreds of ways to network and find good quality leads – your neighbors, friends, alumni networks, and the schools your kids go to can all be great opportunities to network.

But more importantly, don't try to sell right away!

With networking, the focus must be on building a relationship. Always build a relationship first and the sale will come later.

You could also tie-up with someone who already has a list and can do some sort of revenue share with you.

Accountants, lawyers, stock brokers and financial advisers -- all of them might have a client list that might need your services.

Always remember, in networking, it is important that you're a person who provides value.

If you take a favor, figure out a way to return the favor.

Don't be a jerk who's always taking.

Learn to *give*.

Givers will eventually receive. That's how the theory of reciprocity works.

When you help someone, they would want to help you back.

Action Step

Identify your sources for leads. Figure out from where you're going to get your leads. Make a plan and implement it.

Notes:

How to introduce yourself?

Every relationship begins with an introduction. But we very rarely stop and think about how we're going to introduce ourselves to a stranger.

As they say, you never get a second chance to make a first impression.

Usually, your introduction is your first impression and most people can spot a sales person from a distance.

Even when you make a cold call, it's important not to come across as a sales person but, rather, as a friend who's there to solve a problem for the prospect.

If it's a cold call, then the introduction is slightly different. You want to get the benefit out really quick.

I see people make a cold call and they say, "Hi, ahh, uhm, uhm, how are you doing? Are you having a good morning? Can I have two minutes of your time?"

These are all wasting the prospect's time. You want to get the benefit out really quick. And to get the benefit out, I have a simple template for you all.

Here's an example: "Hi, good morning. I'm Robert from Solar Electric. We help small businesses cut their energy costs by 25%. Can I take a few minutes of your time to explain how we do it?"

Right away, you're getting the benefit out to your prospect with just a few words.

Your prospect hears you out and he says, "Okay, these people can save my energy costs by 25%. Let me give him a chance; let me hear him out."

But if you're going to ask your prospect, "Can I have few minutes of your time?," the first thought that comes to the prospect's mind is, "You can have few minutes of my time, but I'd like to know how you're going to benefit me."

Because every single prospect is tuned into a radio station that says, "What's in it for me? What's my benefit?"

Every prospect is thinking, "What's my benefit?" When you call somebody, and if it's a pure cold call, the prospect wants to know the benefit right away. So it's important to give out the benefit in the first five seconds. What I tell people is, the moment you call somebody, be overly polite, be overly humble and be sure to introduce yourself.

You need to have your name, your company's name, your target market and reasons you benefit your target market all on the tip of your tongue and ready to spit out in the first five seconds.

Let's look at the introduction that I just mentioned. When I called I said, "Good morning. I am Robert from Solar Electric." Name is there, Robert. Company name, Solar Electric. "We help small businesses" – small business is my target market — "cut energy costs by 25%" – which is the benefit. "Can I take a few minutes of your time to explain how we did it?" Very simple template.

Your name, company name, target market and the benefit.

You want to mention the target market because you want to let your prospect know that people just like him have benefited from your product.

And once the prospect says, "Okay, sure you can have a few minutes of my time," then you can start with, "If you don't mind me asking you a few questions, do you own a business?"

If he says yes then you say, "Yes. Wow! That's excellent! What kind of products do you sell?"

Once the prospect gives you details about his business, then tell him, "That's wonderful. A similar business like yours saved their energy cost by 25% by using our product and this is how they saved money…"

Tell them a story about how someone just like them saved money using your product.

You also want to find a common ground.

And remember, the purpose of a cold call is to get a sales meeting.

Some people have been able to sell products on a cold call as well, but the odds and probability of selling are very low. So the purpose of a cold call should strictly be to get a meeting.

When you meet someone at a networking event, your introduction is going to be very similar. "Hi, I'm Robert from Solar Electric. We help small businesses cut their energy costs by 25%."

And then, you ask them about themselves like, "How about you? What do you do?"

In a networking event, you're already face-to-face with somebody. So you want to get the other person to talk as much as they can about their business, and about their life. Because when people talk about themselves, their brain activity gets heightened.

This is just a basic template for your introduction.

I'm a great believer in having scripts for everything. Once you have scripts for your introduction, presentation, closing, your follow-up, and everything in place and you've memorized them, you know exactly what to say and you're well prepared.

This is what preparation does for you.

When you have all your scripts in place and you've memorized them, that is called preparation.

One of the qualities of a great sales person is that he's always well prepared.

Action Step

Write down your introduction.

Fill in the blanks below. "I am (your name), (designation), (company name). We help (target market) (benefit)."

Once you write down your introduction, memorize it so that it becomes a part of you. When you introduce yourself, you should come across as fluent and confident. Get ready to fill your calendar with sales meetings!

Notes:

Presentation

Sales people often feel the pressure of closing deals right at the presentation stage.

It's important to be relaxed during the presentation stage and let things flow.

Your primary objective in the presentation phase has to be to identify the prospect's problem, obstacle, needs or wants, and to eventually offer your product or service as a solution to that.

It's important that you don't come across as an interrogator, but more as a friendly person who's genuinely curious to know about the other person.

Always start your presentation on a positive note.

One nice way to start on a positive note is by giving genuine compliments.

It could be as simple as, "You've got a nice office," or, "I like the pen you're using."

But make sure your compliment is *genuine*.

You've got to condition your mind to be a person who looks for the positives in a person.

Every person has negatives.

And it's very easy to see, and focus on, the negatives. But you want to be the person who looks at the positives. Every single person on this planet has positives.

You need to train your mind to look for the good qualities in a person.

Start your presentation with a compliment, and throughout the presentation, you should either be asking questions or telling a relevant story.

People love stories.

Our brain gets activated when we hear stories. Initially, you want to get as many 'yes' answers as possible, so you want to ask obvious questions that will give you a 'yes' answer.

You want to get the prospect to get used to saying yes.

And to get 'yes' answers, all you need to do is ask obvious questions to which you know the answer will be 'yes.'

It could be something like, "Is this your office?" "Yes, it's my office, that's why I'm here."

If he introduces himself as a CEO of the company, you could ask something like, "You're the CEO of the company, right?" He says, 'yes.' "Oh nice, wonderful, marvelous."

Use words like wonderful, brilliant, and marvelous.

These are words that get people excited.

If you want to be an exciting person, you should use exciting words.

Other questions you could ask your prospect include, "Do you want to make more money?"

Most people would say yes to that question!

"Do you want to save money?" Most people want to save money as well.

"Do you want to save time?" All of these are questions that instigate 'yes' answers.

Try to find questions that instigate 'yes' answers.

Along with explaining the benefits of your product, you also want to give them a mental picture of what your product or service can do for them. Remember, people buy feelings. You want to create a feeling in his or her mind about using your product and, for that, you have to give the person a mental picture about your product.

For example, if you're selling a car, you ask your prospect to imagine sitting in that car that has absolutely wonderful leather seating, a beautiful stereo system, and suspensions so smooth that you won't feel a thing while you're driving in the car.

What a mental picture does to a person is that it makes them feel like they're already there, using your product or service.

And when people are already using things, they get emotionally attached to it. So you want to make the prospect feel like he's already using your product or service.

Identify the emotion that you want your prospect to feel and give him a mental picture of using your product.

For example, if you're selling a holiday package to Las Vegas, you'd give them a mental picture of the casinos and the wonderful shows that happen in Vegas.

The same part of the brain that was already there gets activated.

Get on the same page as the prospect. You want to be speaking in the same speed and tone of your prospect. The only exception to that is when your prospect is rude or hostile.

Research has shown that the same part of the brain is activated when two people are on the same page.

Remember, price should never come up until the end of your presentation.

People first need to understand the value of your product or service. Sometimes, people spend more than what they have in mind based on the value you bring to the table.

And remember, you need to start on a positive note; you always need to end on a positive note as well.

People remember the beginning and the end of every presentation. So your beginning has to be positive. The end also needs to be positive.

Tell your prospect it was really nice meeting him, and you would like to meet him again to discuss some of the passions that both of you shared.

In the presentations, you want to casually ask some personal questions. Make sure the personal questions don't seem overly intrusive. Casual questions like, "Do you live around the office?" and "How far do you travel?"

You want to ask these questions to identify a common ground.

So, if both of you went to the same school, church, both of you love the same sports or you have common hobbies, these are all potential points you can connect on.

I remember I met one of my prospects and I was talking to him and I realized that he liked cricket as well.

So I asked him, "Do you play cricket?" He's like, "I play cricket every Sunday."

He even offered for me to join him. So imagine, I got to play cricket with him on the weekends and I got to know him better. In less than a week, I was in his inner circle. Shared passions are a great way to build relationships and, remember, as a sales person your job is to build relationships. If you have a relationship, the sale will eventually happen.

Other presentation tips are:

- Memorize your sales presentation so that it is always at the tip of your tongue.
- Practice, practice, practice!

One of the great qualities of a good sales person is that he has very good knowledge about his product. So you must have good knowledge about your product, otherwise, you're going to struggle through your presentation.

Remember, the sale goes to the person who is well prepared. You want to be that person.

Action Step

Make a list of questions you could ask your prospect.

Each of these questions should uncover their needs, wants and obstacles.

Make a list of relevant stories about your product or service. You can have an archive of relevant stories about your product. Now, every time you go to a sales presentation, you already have a story with you. You don't have to think of one spontaneously.

Notes:

Follow-up

As I mentioned previously, the most important thing in sales is building rapport. Establishing rapport takes time and that's what a follow-up does for you.

One of the top reasons to follow-up is to get to know your prospect better and to strengthen the relationship.

One of the reasons sales people don't follow-up is because they don't know how to follow-up. I believe sales is about adding value to your prospect. And how do you add value to your prospect?

Let's say you've gone over and met a prospect, you've given him a presentation about your product or service and, in the presentation, your job as a sales person is to identify the obstacles and problems of your prospect.

When you get back home, you look over your notes, you identify three or four problems of your prospect, research online and figure out what solutions you can offer your prospect.

Make a small note about it, send him an email and say, "Hey, you know what, we had a discussion yesterday and you said these were your challenges. And here are some solutions for your challenges."

Sometimes, you might find a useful article online. Send them a link and say, "Hey, I came across a useful article for you. Maybe you should check it out."

Once you do that, you can give him a call again.

Give him a call and tell him, "Hey, did you get a chance to read the article I sent you?"

Look at yourself as a consultant who is adding value to your prospect. Your prospect then starts looking at you as an authority, rather than a sales person who's out there to get him.

This is one of the most important ways of following-up.

When you follow-up, you're following up to educate your prospect.

While you follow-up, you also want to find some common ground between you and your prospect.

It could be that you went to the same school or you live in the same neighborhood, or you have common friends.

Another great way of following up that most sales people don't think about is to provide access to your network.

As a sales person, you're meeting many new people every day. You have access to a wide network. Give your prospects access to your network – that's so important! It's very easy to provide access to a network.

You can call your prospect out for a cup of coffee and tell him, "Hey, I'm going to introduce you to three other people."

Instead of calling your prospect out for a one-on-one meeting over coffee, you can call over four or five prospects with you for a cup of coffee at a nice place and you can introduce them to each other. This way, you're giving access to your prospects and you're coming across as a person who's a giver, who's helpful and who's not just out there to make a buck.

This way, you're not providing access to your network to one prospect but to five prospects at a time. This is a fabulous opportunity to build rapport with all five prospects rather than just one.

Sometimes, people overdo it and they call 10, 15, even 20 people. That's a bit too much.

Five is an ideal number. Your coffee dates have to be with five people; that's about it.

Five of your top prospects who you believe could help each other.

This is a silver bullet for a lot of people. Many people I know have tried it; this one person who I explained it to, he tried it and in a month he'd already picked up four new clients. It's a very powerful strategy.

Another thing that seems to be out of fashion, but very effective, are 'thank you' cards. When I was in the retail business, there was a sales person from a local newspaper who used to sell advertising space. After our first meeting, she would stop by every other day at my office and say, "Hey Vinil, I was just passing by. I thought I'd stop by and say hello."

It was a kind gesture. But what she did that caught my attention was when one day I walked into my office and I saw a hand-written thank you note, along with a bottle of wine.

I thought it was a very beautiful gesture. She didn't get business from us immediately, but over a period of time, we became friends, and she eventually got business from me.

There's another story of a client who I got to know over the years. I would meet him very often over a cup of coffee; we would hang out. I never got business from him immediately. In fact, I got business from him after almost two years.

People ask me, "Should I use email or should I use the phone?" I would say both are equally important; I use a strategy called the 3-5-7 email strategy.

When I meet a prospect, I send over an email almost the same day. If I have a meeting today, I email him the same day with a non-pushy, 'non-salesy' email like, "Hey, it was nice meeting you. These are the obstacles and challenges I believe you face in your business. I will do what I can to help you for the next few weeks."

Three days later, I send him another email. This time, with a solution to one of his challenges. And I also give him a call to let him know that I sent him an email, because sometimes emails go into a spam folder, especially with Google. So you want to also give them a call to make sure he received the email.

Another reason for calling them is that you start building rapport and you start sharing some personal information with each other.

And five days later, I send him another solution to another obstacle.

Seven days later, I do the same. And I alternate between email and phone. Once I send an email, 24 hours later, I give him a call.

What I'm trying to do is add value to my prospect at every opportunity I get.

The moment I add value, I get into his inner circle.

Sometimes people ask, "When should I stop following-up?" My answer to that is: you never stop following-up.

If the prospect is busy or he's having a rough time at his work place or you realize that he's never going to purchase your product, during that time, you probably stop calling him up.

But once you've decided not to give him a call, I would say, call him two months after your last attempt because a lot of things change in two months.

The prospect may be ready to buy.

If the prospect is in need of your product, you have to keep following-up all the time. If he's not a prospect, that means he's a suspect, and you realize that he does not require your product, then obviously, you stop following-up.

Action Step

Make a list of old, forgotten leads.

Give them a call or try to set-up a meeting or a Skype call. All these are leads that you may not have followed-up for the last several months.

You'll be surprised when you go through your phone book or places where you've saved your contacts; you'll be surprised that you've missed out on so many wonderful contacts.

For our content writing business, I once went through all my old contacts. I sent all of them an email and I was surprised to see many of our old clients come back into our system.

They had a requirement, but they were procrastinating on the requirement.

They just couldn't pick up the phone and give me a call and say, "This is our requirement."

But when I called them and said, "Hey, you have any requirements?" They're like, "Oh yeah, sure. We have this requirement. We always wanted to call you but we just never did."

Whenever we call up old forgotten leads, we almost always get a response.

Notes:

Handling Objections

Some sales people get intimidated by objections. I want to let you know about an important fact.

Successful sales have more objections than unsuccessful sales.

Why is that?

If somebody is not interested in your product, they're not going to ask you questions.

People are more diplomatic. You tell them, "Do you like the product?" They'll say, "Yeah." "Would you like to buy it?" They'll say, "I'll think about it." And they'll just walk away.

But if somebody is really interested in the product, he's going to ask you a lot of questions. That is why, when somebody raises an objection or asks you a question, smile and be happy about it. Because the more objections you have, the more likely you're going to make a sale.

I'm going to go through some of the most common types of objections that you're going to face.

The first type of objection you could face is, that the prospect will say, "Let me think about it."

Why does a prospect say, "Let me think about it?"

What does he mean by that?

It could mean a few things:

He's not interested in your product and he doesn't want to say no.

Some people are just scared to say no.

There are a few others who are not sure whether to buy or not because they still have certain unanswered objections, or they do not know fully about the product or service.

So when somebody says, "Let me think about it," if you're a really confident person, this is something you need to practice.

Look at the prospect in the eye and say, "Mr. Prospect, there are two kinds of people I come across when they say, 'Let me think about it.' Either they're not interested in the product, or you have some question or some objection that I haven't answered. Is there any question or objection you'd like me to answer?"

Sometimes, the prospect opens up and says, "Yeah, I have so and so questions and objections. What do you think about it?" Then you can get back in the game and start answering his objections.

Other times, the prospect is a slow decision-maker.

He tends to wait, discuss with his spouse, and then make a decision.

But more importantly, when you get to the objection phase, you want to answer as many objections as possible and close the sale right away.

If your prospect walks out of the table after you've handled these objections, the likelihood of you making the sale reduces. You want to somehow handle the objections, get to the closing phase, and close the deal at that moment in time when your prospect is nice and warm.

The moment the prospect goes back home, there's a high likelihood that he might change his mind. So if you've come this far up to the handling objection phase, keep the closing in your mind. Answer objections but try to close your prospect in that specific meeting. Most prospects just have one or two key objections. So, you want to identify these key objections by asking questions.

The other factor is price objections.

Sometimes, your prospect thinks the price is too high.

At that point in time, you want to justify the price based on the value your product brings to the table.

There are times the prospect genuinely does not have the money so you might want to help him out with a payment plan.

Other times, they do have the money but they're not sure if your product is worth the money.

Try to justify the cost of the product based on the value, and the emotional and logical benefits it brings to the table.

Then, there are aggressive objections. Sometimes people are just angry. It's not that they're angry with you, but they're just angry with somebody else who sold them something that they did not want. These are just aggressive objections, and with aggressive objections it's good to just smile and not respond right away.

Let all the anger and aggression come out. Once a prospect has shown his anger and hatred towards you, usually, I've seen that many of the prospects feel bad about it.

I haven't seen somebody who's rude to someone and he feels very good about being rude.

When someone is rude to you, remember, he's giving you power.

Just keep quiet.

Let him unload his anger.

Once he's unloaded his anger, relax and tell him, "Dear Prospect, I understand exactly how you feel. If something like that happened to me, I would feel exactly the same way."

You're showing empathy towards your prospect. He will appreciate that and may even come around.

The next type of objection is the show-off objection.

Sometimes the prospect feels like he knows about the product or services better than you. He would probably walk up to you and say, "You know my cousin worked in this company for 25 years and I know exactly how this works."

With the show-off objection, you've got to feed on the ego of your prospect. What you can do is make him feel like an expert. The easiest way to deal with show-off objections is to ask your prospect, "Sir, I understand you know a lot about the product, can you help me out? What do you think are the benefits of this product?"

Likely, he will go on and on and tell you a lot of benefits about the product. As he keeps telling you the benefits about the product, he is in turn selling himself on the product!

The next type of objection is a general resistance to sales people. Some people just don't like sales people.

How do you break that general resistance towards sales people?

I tell my prospect, "I'm not selling you anything. I'm just going to show you my product, if you don't like it, you don't have to pay for it."

I know it's obvious that if you don't buy it, you don't have to pay for it, but when you say that, prospects generally tend to be a little bit more relaxed.

"I'm not selling you anything," is a sentence that works.

If you don't buy it, you don't pay for it.

That's also something that's very obvious, but it works.

Then, there are your unspoken objections. You're sitting across the table with your prospect and you're asking him a lot of questions.

You're telling him a lot of relevant stories, but he just isn't opening up.

You ask him, "What is your objection? Why is it that you're not going to buy this product? What does it take for me to get the deal?"

He'd be like, "I might have some objections but I'm not letting you know." You will find prospects like that.

Once you've tried to ask question on question on question and have tried to get that unspoken objection out, and you have not succeeded, try this method.

It's called the doorknob method. Somebody discovered it in 1961 and many sales people have used it since.

When your prospect doesn't want to tell you why he does not want to buy your product, take your brochures and your handbooks and your notes, put them in your bag, get up and start walking towards the door.

Just before you're about to open the door, stop, turn towards your prospect and say, "Dear Prospect, just for my understanding, why didn't you want buy my product?"

Usually, when you've packed up and started walking towards the door, the prospect's resistance has dropped, he's now unguarded.

When you turn around and ask him, "Just for my understanding, I'd like to know what was it about my product that you did not like?," there is a high probability that he'll open up and start talking about his objections. Then you come back to the table, sit down quietly, and guess what? You're back in the game.

Then there's the smoke screen objection. What is the smoke screen objection? Basically, the prospect does not believe what you say. So what do you tell your prospect?

Tell your prospect, "Dear Prospect, if we prove it to you, will you take it?"

You're putting him on the spot right there with his objection.

He doesn't believe what you're saying, but if you can prove it, will he take it? Most likely the answer would be yes, or he wouldn't say anything, he would just nod.

If you've done your homework and if your product is really good and you put the right facts into your brochures and in your presentation, it will be easy for you to prove it.

These are some of the basic types of objections you're going to face during a sales presentation.

Action Step

Make a list of obstacles that your prospects may have. They could be real questions that your prospects may have asked you in the past.

Let's call it an FAQ, or frequently asked questions.

Write down possible answers for these questions.

You might also want to contact your sales team to get similar questions and answers so you can anticipate what people may ask you in the future. Preparation is key

Notes:

Closing

Closing is probably one of the most important steps in selling.

I've seen so many sales people who are very good in introducing themselves, who are very good at presentation, they're very good at following-up, and building rapport.

They're kind, nice people who are very good at making friends.

But they struggle with closing.

They're just too embarrassed to ask for a sale.

There's some sort of mental barrier inside of them that inhibits them from going out there and asking for the sale with confidence.

Once you've done a good presentation and you've followed-up, eventually, you have to ask for the sale.

Henry Ford had a very good friend who was an insurance sales person. And when Henry Ford bought insurance from someone else, his friend asked Ford, "Why did you buy insurance from somebody else? Why not from me?" Guess what Henry Ford said? He said, "You didn't ask for it."

One simple step in closing is *asking* for the sale.

You have to be able to go out there and ask for the sale confidently.

You must be enthusiastic about your product.

And when you ask for the sale, you want to ask for it confidently.

I'm going to go through some closing techniques that you can master and perfect.

The first technique is to *ask for the sale*.

Just go out there and ask for the sale.

How do you ask for the sale?

"So, is it a yes or a no?" I assume that everyone wants to buy from me.

While you're doing your presentation, you can also do a *trial close*. In your trial close, you ask your prospect, "What do you think about this?" You'll get a basic idea as to where exactly the prospect is going.

Then there is the *invitation close* where you ask your prospect, "If you like it, why don't you take it?"

Sometimes you have prospects telling you, "I can't afford it." I learned this from a very good sales person. He told me, "Vinil, the moment somebody says, "I can't afford it," tell your prospect, "That's exactly why you should take it."

I know it sounds crazy but if you try it, it just catches the prospect off guard. "That's exactly why you should take it." He starts thinking to himself, "What is this guy trying to tell me? *That's* exactly why I should take it?"

Sometimes, prospects have one key objection. So to counter that key objection, you ask, "What should I do to get the deal today?"

Then we have the *assumption close*. An assumption close is when you just assume the prospect is going to buy your product. So you ask them, "Is it going to be cash or card?"

Another closing technique is to give them a choice. "Is it going to be product A or product B? Which one would you like to take?"

Then, of course, there's my favorite *takeaway close*. Lots of people have fallen for it and lots of people will continue to fall for this takeaway close. It's telling a prospect that they cannot have it.

The moment you tell somebody that they cannot have it, they want to have it. That's human nature and human tendency to want what they cannot have.

Then there's your *touch and feel close*.

Sales people at Xerox, when they make these machines, you don't have to pay for the machine; you just have to pay for the copy.

They would walk into an office and tell them, "Hey, you know what? Let me just leave this machine with you. I'll come back in a week. If you don't like it, I'll take it back."

When it's there in the office and people are seeing it every day, there's a tendency to go ahead and use it.

At the end of the week, when the sales person comes back to the office, you don't have to pay for the entire machine, you just have to pay for the copies that you've used. That's how Xerox works. They moved from a capital expenditure to an operating cost.

Retailers also use a touch and feel close. The customer walks into their store and they like a certain product so the sales person says, "You know what? Take it home. If you don't like it, you can always return it."

The touch and feel close gets your prospects emotionally attached to your product. It's not the physical attachment to something but an emotional attachment to a specific product.

That's what a touch and feel close does for you. You're creating an environment where your prospect could get emotionally attached to your product.

Then there's the *relevant story close*. A relevant story close is a story about someone using your product. If people similar to you are using it, then you want to use it too. That's human tendency.

People want to use the products that their neighbors are using.

People want some sort of consensus that people just like them are also using the product. That's what the relevant story close is. You tell your prospect a story of someone just like them using your product.

Then there's your *pros and cons close*. How does the pros and cons close work? Write down the pros of your product. Once you've finished writing the pros of your product, hand it over to your prospect and tell him, "Mr. Prospect, now why don't you write the cons of the product?"

Most people won't go beyond one or two cons. When someone sees the benefits of a product, there's a higher likelihood of you closing the sale.

Then there's the *summary close*.

Summary close is nothing but you summarizing your entire presentation.

Tell them, "In the last one hour, this is what we've discussed. These are the features that you'd like. These are the benefits of these features." Also give them a mental picture of how your product is going to change his life.

Then there is the *order close*. Some companies have an order form. In the order form, just make a note of whatever products your prospect likes. Your prospect's looking at a specific product, you sit down with him and start entering each product in your order book.

If your prospect says, "Hey, hold on. I haven't decided to buy any product yet so don't make a bill." Tell your prospect, "Mr. Prospect, this is not a bill. This is just an order book. At the end of it all, if you don't like it, I'll just rip it apart and throw it away. Don't worry about it."

These are just some of the methods of *closing*.

I tell my coaching clients, "Always plan your closing. Make a list of statements you're going to tell your prospect at closing."

Practice your closing as much as you can.

Try it on friends, and colleagues. A few things to remember when you're closing:

- Always close with enthusiasm and belief in your product.
- Have confident expectations. Expect your prospect to buy your product.

Action Step

Make a list of closing statements where you are specifically asking for the sale.

Hello, Prospect. Is it going be a yes, or a yes?

Would it be product A or product B?"

Memorize these closing statements. They should become part of you. After every presentation you must be able to ask for the sale confidently. If you don't ask, the universe will not give it to you.

Notes:

Creating Energy

One of the most important qualities of a sales professional is energy.

Can energy be created? I believe it can.

Sometimes, an individual walks into a room, and suddenly everyone is infected by his energy. How is that possible?

For many people, it happens subconsciously.

They subconsciously learn the trick of creating great energy.

Many of us might have to work a little bit harder to create that sort of energy. It's not that difficult to create energy. I think energy is very important. There's a little exercise that you can try on your team. It might sound a bit cheesy, but it works.

Every morning, just before work, get your team together in a huddle. Play some high energy music. It needs to be loud, but not so loud that it will break your ear drums. But it needs to be just loud enough.

Make your team either jump or dance; something enough to break a sweat.

Usually it's just about five to seven minutes.

Then turn off the music and yell, "Who's the best team player in the world? Say I!"

"Who's gonna break all sales record(s) today? Say I!"

If you don't have a team, do this exercise by yourself.

Just play high energy motivational music, and keep jumping up and down, or dance.

Once you finish dancing, say, "Who's the best sales person in the world? Say I!" Shout, "I!"

"Who's gonna break all sales records today? Say I!"

This might sound overboard for some people who've never done this. But it's important to start each day on a positive note. This exercise increases your adrenaline and releases endorphins in your body. Endorphins are happy chemicals; they really make you feel happy! If your team starts on a happy, energetic and positive note each day, you increase your chances of selling more.

Personally, I think team meetings are getting boring. Spice it up with some music. I think music is a fabulous way to create good energy.

Action Step

Pull your team together in a huddle and create energy by doing the exercise I just mentioned.

Notes:

Your Value

Let's say you're Sales Person A and your competitor is Sales Person B. Both of you sell the exact same product. Why should a prospect buy from you rather than your competitor?

The first value you bring to the table and the way you differentiate yourself from other sales people are your key insights.

What are key insights? Key insights provide information that is relevant to your prospect in making a good decision.

Lot of the things that we believe is obvious may not be obvious to your prospect. You're dealing with your product on a day-to-day basis.

You know your industry very well.

Through the course of your job, you're doing a lot of research and identifying new things.

You've met over a hundred prospects, explained to them about your product, about the industry, and you've gotten to know a lot of things.

The information about your industry and your products become obvious to you. But they're not obvious to your prospect.

Sometimes your prospect is just a beginner, and many of the things that you're saying might be new information. Don't undervalue the knowledge that you bring to the table.

Your first value proposition that you bring to the table are key insights – information that is going to help your prospect make good decisions.

The next value you bring to the table is your own unique perspective.

What is perspective?

Perspective is the way you look at things.

Remember, your prospect is looking for help to make a good decision.

Great sales people help the prospect navigate choices. They also give them their perspective about a specific product.

So, it's important that you bring your perspective to the table as well.

Make the prospect look at a specific product or service in many different ways.

If a prospect says, "This is too expensive," you can tell the prospect, "Listen, you're going to use the product for the next 10 years.

If you calculate the price that you're paying, it's a few extra cents a day.

Would you want to sacrifice so much comfort for a few cents a day?"

That's bringing perspective to the table.

Sometimes, you go to a restaurant and you don't know what to order.

You ask the waiter, who is also a sales person in some way, "What should I buy? What is good out here?"

The waiter says, "Everything out here is good."

The reason the prospect asks you what he should buy means he wants help in making a decision.

So you ask questions, identify his likes and dislikes, and recommend a product that you believe he will like based on the information you've received from him.

The biggest fear among prospects is that they don't want to make bad decisions.

They want to avoid making bad decisions.

You, as a sales person, help your prospects make good decisions with the value you bring to the table.

That's another job of yours as a sales person.

While going through this course, you may have realized that sales is a fairly responsible job. Sometimes you have a lot of power and with power comes responsibility. You want to be a responsible sales person who helps prospects make good decisions.

The reason you don't want your prospects to make bad decisions is because you make it bad for every other sales person.

I sell marketing services and sometimes I go meet a prospect, and they're like, "Vinil, we've tried a lot of these things. We hired this agency and we hired that agency and you know what? They screwed us over. I'm not sure if we want to go with an agency ever again."

What this prospect has is called buyer's remorse.

He is discontent with the product he's bought. You don't want to make it difficult for the entire industry.

You want to be a responsible person who helps the prospect make good decisions.

Another value you bring to the table as a sales person is that you help the prospect justify the cost of the product.

In one of my seminars, somebody asked me, "Are sales people going to be out of business in the next 10 years because machines and computer programs are going to be doing all the selling?" Come to think about it, it sounded a little bit scary, but I don't think sales people will ever go out of business.

In my business, I've seen that even though people purchase my products online, when they deal with a human element, the value of a product always goes up.

I do believe sales people have a big, massive responsible role to play in the world of business.

I still believe sales people make or break a business and it's time we started getting good quality sales people in the market.

Action step

Write down your value as a sales person.

It could be anything; even your pleasant and humble personality, knowledge about your industry, your ability to connect with your prospect on a personal level, key insights, etc.

Write down whatever comes to mind. You want to be clear about the value you bring to the table.

Notes:

Offers

A very good friend of mine who is a master salesman says, "Sales is all about offers."

When I started off in the Marketing Services business, I didn't realize how important offers were. I tried to customize my services for every single client, and customizing is extremely time consuming; it's very hard to figure out what exactly your client wants. So, it's best to standardize services.

I'm a big believer in standardized products and services because they help you scale up very quickly.

So, after many years, I started creating packages for my clients – service-based packages.

And every now and then, I kept throwing in offers. And there are four things I realized about making offers work for you.

The first thing is, your offer has to be very clear for your prospect to understand.

I keep going through my spam folder to figure out what people are doing, because that's where most offers end up. And majority of the time, I just can't figure out what people are selling.

Don't make your offers so complicated that people cannot figure out what you're selling.

What you're selling has to be absolutely clear in the offer.

Your prospects should understand what they're going to get if they avail the offer.

First thing is *clarity*.

Get clarity and make sure your prospect understands the offer. So make your offer very easy to understand – you buy one, you get one free. Easy, simple to understand.

Number two: Make your offer irresistible. If you're going to make an offer at a 5% discount, it doesn't make any sense.

Not irresistible at all.

You want an offer to have a substantial discount.

In some industries, 10% is a substantial discount.

In some industries, even 40% is not a substantial discount. So you need to figure out what sort of discount you could give your prospect.

Sometimes it's not even a discount.

I've seen people not give a discount but, rather, they throw in bonuses. And sometimes, the bonus is far more valuable than the product itself.

Number three: You want your offer to be time sensitive.

You cannot throw in an offer that's going to last forever. I throw in offers where the offer is valid only for that specific day, and the prospect gets an email saying, "The offer is valid for today only." It creates a sense of urgency that they need to take action *now*.

I've seen so many software companies, even retail stores throwing up offers and saying, "The offer is valid only for today." The offer has to be time sensitive.

Number four: Give the offer only to a limited number of people.

You can position your offer in such a manner that only the first five people get this offer. Beyond that, nobody else gets this offer.

So these are the four ways you can make your offer irresistible for your prospect.

Remember, about 30% of your success depends on creating great offers.

Action Step

Create an irresistible offer for any of your products or services.

Promote this offer to your prospects.

You can promote them via email or, you can give them a call.

Ideally, it's best to email them, then give them a call and follow-up on the offer.

Make sure the offer is valid only for a limited time. It could be just for one day, three days, a week, or a month. But make sure the offer is valid only for a *limited* period of time.

Notes:

How to be a Master Networker

Business networking can be a very cost-efficient way of generating leads and closing sales. A lot of people have built their entire businesses around networking alone.

Some of the places where you can network include your local chamber of commerce, business conferences – there are a lot of summits happening all over the world - and meet-up groups. In fact, many meet-up groups are free of cost.

You can join a meet-up group where your ideal customer hangs out. That's why it's very important for you to know your ideal customer.

In the previous lessons, we discussed how to identify your ideal customer.

I hope you've identified your ideal customer.

Once you've identified your ideal customer, all you need to do is to figure out where your ideal customer hangs out.

He could be hanging out at local bars, specific meet-up groups, trade shows, or at business conferences.

There are also several groups like BNI, where people help you give referrals and people help you get referrals.

The important thing is to identify where exactly your ideal customer hangs out.

Once you identify where your ideal customer hangs out, you can hang out at those places too.

This increases your chances of meeting your idea customer. And remember, the most important thing about business networking is to build relationships.

I see a lot of people who go to business conferences and all they do is exchange business cards.

They give out business cards, they collect business cards, and the next day, they send them a long email about what products and services they offer.

Right away they say, "Hey I met you at the conference and these are the products and services I offer. Would you like to purchase some of them, or do you know anybody who would purchase these products and services?"

That's a very *wrong* way of networking.

The whole idea about networking is about building relationships.

I would go further to say business networking means business relationships.

How do you build these relationships?

First and foremost, you've got to have a great introduction.

In the previous lessons we've spoken about how to introduce yourself, and I hope you've written down your introduction and that you're very confident about introducing yourself.

Once you've introduced yourself, ask the person who you've met at the business conference about themselves. People have a heightened brain activity when they talk about themselves. So, get people to talk about themselves, and ask open-ended questions.

Questions that begin with a 'Why' or a 'How' are usually open ended questions. You want to be asking questions that begin with a 'why' or a 'how', rather than 'what' or a 'when.' This is something you need to keep in mind when asking questions.

Dig deeper.

Ask them further questions about their story, about themselves – why did they start their business? What is the real motivation behind it? Remember, in networking, you're either asking questions or telling stories. Because stories create a heightened brain activity.

People ask me, "Where do you get your stories from?" It's very simple. Ask yourself, "What's the most interesting story I've ever heard?"

You must have heard several stories and most people have read so many stories.

All you need to do is sit down and ask yourself, what's the most interesting story you've ever read?

Make a note of that story.

Tell that story again to yourself.

Figure out *why* it was interesting, then ask yourself, "What are the turning points in my life?"

Identify all the turning points in your life.

Every person has had turning points in their lives. Then ask yourself, "What was the most challenging moment in my life and how did I overcome it?"

People love stories where you overcome an obstacle or a challenge.

Identify what those moments in your life are.

Every single person has had challenging moments in their life. Identify what those challenging moments are, and identify how you overcame them. That's also another story.

You must have also heard many funny stories.

Make a note of those funny stories as well.

I've got some funny stories as well. I'll tell you one of my stories. It's both funny and embarrassing, but I will tell you that story at the risk of embarrassing myself.

I was in Miami at a night club; I used to live in Boca Raton, Florida at that time. It's a 45 minute drive to Miami.

My roommate, his girlfriend and I went to this night club in Miami. I met a girl from Norway.

We became friends at that night club and then I asked if I could buy her a drink. She's like, "Yeah, sex on the beach." And I was like, "Right now?" And she said, "Right now." Then I realized, sex on the beach was a cocktail drink that was on the menu.

It didn't really mean she wanted to have sex on the beach.

I tell this story to a lot of people and now that I'm a little bit older it's kind of embarrassing. But during those days, it was a funny story.

People remember the story even after 15 years.

The thing about funny stories and interesting stories is that it builds memories and people remember you over a period of time.

That's what business networking is all about.

It's about telling those funny stories and creating those memorable moments.

You want to be known as the guy who's got all these interesting and funny stories, because people love stories. And that's how you get people to open up; by telling them stories and asking them about their stories.

Remember, it's not just about you. It's also about them. So, your job is not just to be entertaining, but to also make the other person look entertaining and interesting. And you do that by asking questions.

Other intellectual conversations you can have with people are about the books that you've read. Recently, when I was at a business conference, I had a discussion with this person about Jack Welch's book, 'Winning.'

The moment we started talking about the book, we hit it off.

We realized we had similar interests, similar passions – I was an entrepreneur, he was an entrepreneur, and we both are passionate about growing our businesses.

Things like this create that common ground between you and your prospect.

You don't want to talk about any gossip or anything negative. Always talk positive. It's important to position yourself as a positive person, who talks good about people and sees good in people.

Action Step

Write down the most interesting story you've ever read.

Then write down all of the major turning points in your life.

Then sit down and write all the challenges and moments in your life and how you overcame them.

And then, write down a funny story you've heard. Anything funny, just write that down.

If you have two or three interesting stories, write them down. If you have several turning points in your life, write them down as well.

And also, write down everything about your collection of books.

I'm sure many of you have read a lot. Write down a list of books you've read, and all the interesting things you've learned from those books.

Now, you have a whole archive of stories and when you meet somebody at a networking event, you're not short of content.

You have a lot of content in terms of interesting stories, turning points, challenging moments, funny stories, and a whole list of books. You won't be short of topics!

Notes:

Breaking Mental Barriers

I believe sales is more of a mental game than a technical game. Most of the game is played in our heads rather than with our prospect.

I played tennis when I was younger and my coach always told me, "You are your own toughest opponent to beat."

A lot of people end up beating themselves. They lose the battle even before they get on to the battlefield because the battle is fought in your head rather than on the field.

And that's so true for sales as well. We all have a lot of mental barriers that are inhibiting us from moving ahead.

They make us get stuck in life.

Because of these mental barriers, we're not just stuck in life, we're also stuck in sales, our careers, and in a lot of other areas.

A very smart articulate trainer I know struggled to sell his training programs because he had very strong inhibitions against sales.

He was too scared to sell, or to ask for the sale.

He would freeze up when it came to asking people for money.

In fact, all our lives, we've been told negative stories about sales like, sales people are bad, they're loud, they're obnoxious and they lie a lot.

Many of these stories have an impact on us and we're not even aware of it.

As I mentioned in my previous lessons, as adults, we have the power to change our stories through conscious behavior.

We talked about affirmation in our previous lessons.

There's strong research that has shown that questions are extremely powerful; even more powerful than affirmations. They force your mind to find answers and challenge your beliefs.

It's very important to be aware of your beliefs and your value systems as well.

Action Steps

Ask yourself the following questions:

Is sales important to the success of my company? If yes, am I giving it as much importance as I should?

What if I increase my sales conversions by just 5%? Will it benefit my business?

Do I have any mental barriers or inhibitions in sales? If yes, what are they? Are these inhibitions reasonable?

What am I doing to change my negative beliefs? Will changing my negative beliefs benefit me?

These are the questions you need to ask yourself.

Find answers for them within you.

And the moment you're clear about your beliefs, your mental barriers, sales becomes much more easier.

Notes:

Referrals

Once upon a time, my entire business worked on referrals. I'll show you a simple process that you can use to increase your referral rate.

Number one: Be brilliant at your job.

The reason you want to be brilliant at your job is because people like to refer vendors who are good at what they do.

Everybody wants to give out referrals.

It's not that your satisfied customers do not want to give out referrals, they *want* to give out referrals – it's just that we don't ask for it.

So, step number one, you've got to be brilliant at what you do, you've got to exceed expectations, and focus on the one thing that you do best.

You want to become well-known for that one thing that you do best. So ask yourself that question: "What is that one thing that I do best that my competition is not very good at?"

Number two: Share your ideal customer profile with your network. Let your network know who your ideal customers are.

Number three: Referrals are not just about receiving, but they are also about giving.

You must learn to be a giver.

Once you are a giver, people are more likely to give back. That's how the theory of reciprocity works – when you help somebody, other people want to help you back.

Number four: Make a list of your top 20 customers. These should be customers who are absolutely satisfied with your product or services; these are the ones who are more willing to give out referrals.

Number five: Ask from a satisfied customer. You want to ask for a referral with confidence. And the best time to ask for a referral is just after someone has complimented your work.

Once they've complimented your work, ask them in a polite but confident manner.

Tell them, "Hey, do you think you can refer your friends or colleagues or anyone else who might be interested in our services?" Then, tell them who your ideal customer is.

And once you get referrals, you want to call up the person who your client has referred as soon as possible.

Once you get a sale with a person who your client has referred, send them a thank you note.

You want to send them a thank you note and a nice gift along with the note. The gift could be something as simple as a box of chocolates.

Customers appreciate it when you thank them for the referrals they have given you. It puts you in their good books.

If you want to be a sales person who's memorable, send a thank you note along with a nice gift.

Action Step

Make a list of your top 20 ecstatic customers.

Give them a casual call to see how they're doing and if they're facing any challenges with your product.

Get feedback from them.

Then, ask them for a referral in a polite but confident manner.

And then follow-up on those referrals. Let the person know that they were referred by XYZ person who's already a satisfied customer of yours.

Use the sample script below. You can tweak it, or create your own.

"Hi Jennifer, I'm Robert, Sales Manager at Solar Electric. I got your referral from Sonia Malar. I've been doing business with Sonia for quite some time, and she said you might be interested in cutting your energy costs by at least 25%. I'd be honored if you can give me a 10 minute meeting at your convenience. If not, I can even explain how we can save your energy costs over the phone."

Script Template

"Hi <Prospect's name>, I am <Your Name>, <Designation>, <Company Name>. I got your referral from <referring client>. I've

been doing business with <referring client> for quite some time, and she said you might be interested in <benefit>. I'd be honored if you can give me a 10 minute meeting at your convenience. If not, I can even explain <what your product does for the prospect> over the phone."

Notes:

Landing Pages

You may have heard the terms landing pages, squeeze pages, and sales letters.

The objective of a landing page is to either generate leads, or to close a sale.

You may have seen some of my landing pages.

I have a landing page where I give out a seven day e-course.

On the landing page, my benefit is very clearly listed. I've asked my readers if they would like a free seven day e-course.

They enter their email, phone number, and they click on the 'submit' button.

The moment they click on the submit button, their details automatically go to my email software and they get a welcome message saying, *"Thank you for enrolling for the seven day free e-course. Over the next seven days, you will get one lesson a day."*

And I also tell them that they will be subscribed to my mailing list.

So, that's how my auto-responders are set-up and it's pretty much automated.

You could set-up similar auto-responders for your business where you could give out either a free demo, or a free twenty-minute consulting session.

The word 'free' works very well in marketing.

I believe it's very important to set up a landing page. You've got to have the benefits listed on the landing page.

Along with the benefits, sometimes it's good to give out a free special report – it could be a case study, case studies are very good.

You can give out white papers as well. A white paper is a report that addresses a common problem of the entire industry.

The conversion rate of people on your landing pages are much higher if you give out something free.

Figure out what you can give away for free.

Even though it took us a long time to write the e-book, we give it away free of cost.

When you give away something for free, it entices people to give out their information.

That's the purpose of giving away a free gift.

I've also seen people give away free consulting.

If you're considered an expert in your industry and in your field, you can give away a twenty-minute consulting session for free and after the consulting session, you can always pitch them your product.

I'm going to discuss six ways in which you can make your landing pages more effective.

One of them is, you should talk directly to your prospective customer. In the previous lesson, we discussed about identifying your target market. You want to profile your ideal customer.

The reason you want to do that is you need to know who you're talking to.

Visualize who your ideal customer is and write your copy specifically for that ideal customer.

The second way to make your landing pages great is you want to touch a pain point; what is that one obstacle that your customer wants to solve?

Every product is a solution to a problem.

What is the problem your prospect is facing and how is your product a solution to your problem?

You want your landing page to touch on your pain point.

Number three: You want your landing page to just have one objective.

You're either acquiring leads, or making a sale, or just trying to increase inquiries for your product.

Whatever it is, make sure you have *one* objective.

The biggest mistake with landing pages is trying to do too many things at once.

I suggest that you pick one objective and if you have several different objectives, have different landing pages for each of those objectives.

Number four: Very clearly state the benefits.

If you want to increase your conversions in terms of how many people give you their information, you want to very clearly state the benefits.

Tell the customer what will happen if they buy your product, or tell the customer what will happen if they enter their information and click on the submit button.

Are they going to get something free of cost, in some way to become bigger, stronger, happier, funnier?

Figure out what benefit a customer is going to get by giving out their information.

So, very clearly state the benefits of your product. You could also very clearly state the benefits of subscribing to your mailing list.

Number five: This is the big deal.

I see a lot of websites make this mistake.

That is, they have too many shiny objects all over the place.

Shiny objects are distractions.

What do I mean by that?

When somebody gets on to your landing page, you want them to enter their information and click on submit.

What I see in a lot of websites is that there are too many columns, sometimes you have three columns, four columns. The reader does not know where to look.

You want to make it easy for your reader by having nice and clean landing pages. Try to have as few distractions as possible.

And number six: You want to have a very clear call to action.

Landing pages should tell the reader exactly what to do.

There has to be a clear call to action – it could be asking them to sign up on a mailing list, or even asking for a sale.

Some formatting tips for landing pages, I'd say make it easy for the reader with headings and sub-headings.

The purpose of the heading is to entice your reader to read the first line.

The first line should entice him to read the next, and so on.

People don't usually read word-for-word of an article. They just scan through the article.

You want to have sub-headings so, that when people scan through, you still catch their attention with sub-headings.

Your copy should also have short paragraphs.

Long paragraphs can be very intimidating, and people may not want to read long paragraphs.

So you want to keep your paragraphs short – ideally not more than three sentences. Small chunks of information are more digestible for the reader.

And you want your fonts to be readable; they shouldn't be too large or too small. If it's too small, it's difficult for them to read it.

If it's too large also, it gets difficult to read comfortably.

Another method to make your copy more readable is bullet points and numbered lists.

It just makes the copy more organized. A common question that I get is, "What if I don't have good copywriting skills?"

I believe copywriting is a specialized skill. The copy on your website is too important to be done by a novice.

If you don't have the skills, find someone who's a really good copywriter. I believe a good copywriter is worth every penny.

Landing pages are a great way to acquire leads and make a sale. Sometimes the most important pages on your website are your landing pages.

You don't really need a programmer or a designer to create nice landing pages for you.

You can do it with almost no programming skills. There are a lot of softwares around that can create landing pages for you. You don't even need a web domain in many cases.

The two softwares I use to make landing pages are Unbounce and Lead Pages.

Although Lead Pages is a little bit more expensive, I like Lead Pages better than Unbounce.

Along with the landing page, you also want to get auto-responders. Some of the most common and popular auto-responders are Awebber, Mailchimp, and Getresponse.

The advantage with Getresponse is that they have templates to help you create landing pages.

Although most of the landing pages on Getresponse are fairly basic, they're still useful for somebody who's just starting off.

So if you're starting off and you don't want to spend too much money, you can start off with Getresponse.

If you want a more robust and sophisticated landing page, Leadpages is really good.

Action Step

Sign up for an email marketing software like Mailchimp, Awebber or Getresponse. Set-up your welcome email and your auto-responders.

As I mentioned earlier, Getresponse offers landing pages as well. If you don't want to go that route, you can sign-up on

Leadpages and Unbounce and create a landing page for your business and integrate it with your mailing list software and set-up your landing pages and email auto-responders.

I've also come across people who don't want to set-up their own auto-responders and landing pages.

In that case, you can hire a professional to do it for you.

In fact, my company helps people set-up landing pages and auto-responders. If you're interested in this service, you can visit http://ceohangout.com/services and purchase one of our packages.

Notes:

Habits of Successful Sales People

I congratulate you for coming this far in your training program.

Give yourself a pat on the back.

This lesson is about the habits that are important for top performing sales people. I believe habits make a person, and success in life is determined mainly by our habits.

Habit number one: Don't just focus on achieving your quota.

Try to set big, unreasonable and unpractical goals.

I'm a big believer in the law of attraction.

The universe will give you what you ask from it.

Look at the biggest and greatest inventions in the world.

When you want something badly enough, the universe will find a way to give it to you.

When you set an unpractical goal, you're setting a goal that nobody has ever achieved before.

That doesn't mean that you can't achieve that unpractical goal.

Try to set a goal of 10x your quota.

People think this is something that cannot be done or will not be done, but I do suggest that you try that because I've seen top performing sales people do exactly that. They set extremely big and audacious goals and they just go for it.

They don't think about whether it's possible or not.

And when you set big and audacious goals, the universe will find a way to help you get there.

It may not happen immediately, but you'll be surprised that sometimes, big, audacious goals do happen, and don't be scared to fail.

It's okay to fail when you set big, audacious goals.

But what if you succeed?

One of my mentors said, "Vinil, set a goal that will blow your mind off if you achieve it." That's what I encourage you all to do; to set goals that will blow your mind off.

Habit number two: Get into the habit of generating leads and building relationships.

Sales is all about building relationships. You've got to always keep looking around you to find new people and to build relationships.

Spend 80% of your time on generating new leads and 20% of your time nurturing your existing leads.

Habit number three: This is a very important habit. Build in time for yourself and for your family.

You want to spend time away from work to recharge your batteries.

Go on a vacation at least once a year.

Do things that you enjoy every single day.

Take your hobbies very seriously. The most successful people take their hobbies very seriously; you should too.

Do something fun and interesting every single day because if you are only working most of the time, one day you'll wake up and you'll ask yourself, "What's the point in working so hard?" Focus on doing things outside of work.

Don't live to work, work to live. That's what I was told a long time ago and I encourage you to follow this principle of enjoying your life.

Habit number four: Invest in learning new things. Successful people are learning something new every single day.

Even 15 minutes of trying to learn something new can be very beneficial.

Learning is good, and learning is sometimes enjoyable as well. But what is even more fun is taking action.

Habit number five: The top performing sales people are focused on revenue-generating activities rather than routine, administrative tasks. Shuffling papers, filing – all these are administrative tasks that are time consuming.

Delegate these tasks and free up your time. You should try and focus the majority of your time on revenue-generating activities.

Habit number six: Set high standards for yourself. Maintain a high level of integrity. Look to benefit your prospect, get into the habit of being a person of value.

Habit number seven: You want to wake up and start your day at the same time every day. Have a plan for your entire day.

Habit number eight: I believe life is a beautiful gift and we don't take enough time to appreciate our lives. I do believe gratitude is important. When you wake up in the morning, get into the habit of being grateful for this beautiful gift called life.

Habit number nine: Focus on what you want rather than what you don't want.

It is very easy for us to become very negative about everything that is happening around us.

I encourage you to instead focus on all the wonderful things that are happening to you, rather than the negative things.

If you focus on the negative things, your attention and energy is focused on what you don't want rather than what you want. So, the whole idea is to focus your time, energy, and your attention to what you really want.

I encourage you to develop these nine habits and make them a part of your life.

Action Step

Write down every single thing what you're grateful for.

It could be anything – it could be the beautiful sunshine, the wonderful house you live in or the love of your spouse.

Notes:

Conclusion

Life is all about taking action and attracting the things that you want.

The purpose of writing this book is to help you do just that. Don't underestimate the power of little, incremental steps.

I wanted to put together a course and a book where my audience can make visible progress each day.

I've seen people who sometimes read a book or take a course, and struggle to implement the concepts. My purpose is to add action steps so my readers can see visible progress each day.

It's been a wonderful experience putting this together, and hearing from so many people from all over the world.

I wish you all the success and happiness in the world.

For a list of my books, coaching programs and to connect with me, please visit http://vinilramdev.com

Index

A

activities, 16, 21, 22, 23, 24, 27, 101
AdWords, 36
affirmations, 12, 13, 14, 15, 86
Awebber, 97

B

Bruce Lee, 18
business, 5, 6, 12, 25, 29, 32, 35, 36, 37, 38, 41, 42, 43, 52, 53, 54, 74, 76, 79, 80, 81, 83, 86, 88, 90, 91, 93, 98

C

Cadillac, 11, 31
careers, 4, 85
CEO, 2, 45
challenge, 5, 6, 17, 22, 82, 86
charitable, 5
cheerleader, 14
children, 11
Closing, iii, 34, 63
competitors, 10
conference, 25, 80, 81, 83
conflict, 8
copywriting, 96
customer, 28, 30, 66, 79, 80, 89, 90, 94, 95

D

decision, 6, 7, 24, 57, 71, 72, 73
discount, 77
discoveries, 14
distractions, 95
download, 36

E

energy, 12, 41, 42, 69, 70, 90, 102
enthusiasm, 67
entrepreneur, 4, 5, 6, 12, 83

Index

F

FAQ, 62
focus, 12, 16, 17, 22, 23, 35, 36, 38, 45, 88, 99, 101, 102
follow-up, 43, 50, 51, 78, 90
free, 93
funds, 4

G

Generation, 34
genuine, 44, 45
Getresponse, 97
goals, 14, 16, 17, 19, 22, 30, 99, 100

H

habit, 5, 23, 100, 101, 102
Habit, 99, 100, 101, 102
habits, 20, 99, 102
handbook, 8
happiness, 103
Henry Ford, 63

I

implement, 5, 22, 39, 103
inmails, 37
integrity, 6, 8, 101
introduce, iii, 40, 41, 43, 51, 52, 81

J

judge, 8
justify, 58, 74

L

landing, 36, 37, 92, 93, 94, 95, 96, 97, 98
Leadpages, 97, 98

lifetime, 7, 25, 26
LinkedIn, 35, 37

M

machine, 14, 65
Mailchimp, 97
marketing, 4, 27, 37, 73, 93, 97
Mason Currey, 24
mechanism, 23
mental, 12, 20, 21, 46, 47, 63, 67, 85, 86, 87
methodology, 7
missed, 54
moment, 11, 12, 13, 17, 18, 23, 41, 54, 58, 64, 65, 82, 83, 87, 92

N

networking, 25, 35, 38, 42, 43, 79, 80, 81, 83, 84
newspaper, 4, 35, 52
note, 7, 44, 47, 51, 52, 67, 70, 81, 82, 89, 90

O

objection, 56, 57, 58, 59, 60, 61, 65
objections, 56, 57, 58, 59, 60, 61
objective, 44, 92, 94
offers, 76, 77, 78, 97
owners, 29, 32

P

philosophy, 7, 8
positive, 9, 12, 13, 14, 15, 44, 47, 70, 83
practice, 14, 18, 48, 57
presentation, 43, 44, 45, 47, 48, 49, 50, 61, 63, 64, 66, 68
principles, 7
productivity, 16, 24

Index

profession, 10
prospect, 7, 32, 40, 41, 42, 44, 45, 46, 47, 48, 50, 51, 52, 53, 54, 57, 58, 59, 60, 61, 64, 65, 66, 67, 71, 72, 73, 74, 75, 76, 77, 78, 83, 85, 91, 94, 101

Q

questions, 32, 42, 45, 46, 47, 48, 56, 57, 58, 60, 61, 62, 73, 81, 83, 86

R

referrals, 80, 88, 89, 90
relationship, 7, 38, 40, 48, 50
reward, 17, 22, 23

S

Sales, 1, iii, 4, 34, 35, 44, 65, 71, 76, 90, 99, 100
Schedule, iii, 24, 26
scripts, 43
self-image, 10, 11, 12, 13
shampoo, 31

strategy, 52, 53
successful, 5, 6, 10, 11, 13, 18, 31, 101

T

target, 28, 29, 30, 36, 41, 42, 43, 94
team, 12, 21, 27, 62, 69, 70
Template, 90

V

value, 6, 7, 9, 38, 47, 50, 51, 53, 54, 58, 71, 72, 73, 74, 75, 86, 101
visual, 13

W

Warren Buffet, 7, 24
WhatsApp, 21
workshop, 21

X

Xerox, 65

www.ingramcontent.com/pod-product-compliance
Lightning Source LLC
Chambersburg PA
CBHW061146180526
45170CB00002B/637